SCIENTIFIC AMERICAN EDUCATIONAL PUBLISHING

HOLIDAY SCIENCE

10 FUN CHEMISTRY AND FOOD SCIENCE PROJECTS

BRING SCIENCE HOME

Published in 2023 by Scientific American Educational Publishing in association with
The Rosen Publishing Group 29 East 21st Street, New York, NY 10010

Contains material from Scientific American, a division of Springer Nature America, Inc., reprinted by permission as well as original material from The Rosen Publishing Group.

First Edition

Editor: Theresa Emminizer
Designer: Rachel Rising

Activity on page 5 by Science Buddies (January 1, 2015); page 9 by Science Buddies (February 12, 2015); page 13 by Science Buddies (March 12, 2015); page 19 by Science Buddies (March 21, 2013); page 27 by Science Buddies (May 8, 2014); page 33 by Science Buddies (June 12, 2014); page 37 by Science Buddies (July 3, 2014); page 43 by Science Buddies (August 14, 2014); page 47 by Science Buddies (October 23, 2014); page 55 by Science Buddies (December 1, 2013).

Photo Credits: pp. 3, 5, 8, 9, 11. 12. 13 , 16, 17, 19, 24, 27, 31, 32, 33, 35. 36, 37, 40, 43, 45, 46. 47, 51. 55. 58, 59 cve iv/Shutterstock.com; pp. 4, 5, 9, 13, 19, 27, 33, 37, 43, 47, 55 Anna Frajtova/Shutterstock.com.

All illustrations by Continuum Content Solutions

Cataloging-in-Publication Data
Names: Scientific American.
Title: Holiday science: 10 fun chemistry and food science projects / Scientific American.
Description: New York : Scientific American Educational, 2023. | Series: Bring science home| Includes bibliographic information, glossary and index.
Identifiers: ISBN 9781684169818 (pbk) | ISBN 9781684169825 (library bound) | ISBN 9781684169832 (ebook)
Subjects: LCSH: Experiments-- Juvenile literature | Holidays-- Juvenile literature | Science projects-- Juvenile literature
Classification: LCC Q182.3 S35 2023 | DDC 507 --dc23

Manufactured in the United States of America

CONTENTS

THESE ACTIVITIES INCLUDE SCIENCE FAIR PROJECT IDEAS.

INTRODUCTION

Holidays are the most special times of the year. They bring us together. They give us a reason to celebrate. Whether you're looking for a spooky new activity for your Halloween party or a Mother's Day gift idea, you'll find it here. Add fun and flavor to your holiday traditions with these entertaining and educational experiments. You'll create holiday memories to last a lifetime!

Projects marked with include a section called Science Fair Project ideas. These ideas can help you develop your own original science fair project. Science fair judges tend to reward creative thought and imagination, and it helps if you are really interested in your project. You will also need to follow the scientific method. See page 61 for more information about that.

Soupy Science

Investigate How Dried Beans Absorb Water

MAKE A TASTY NEW YEAR'S TREAT!

PROJECT TIME

45-60 minutes

KEY CONCEPTS

- Food science
- Water
- Absorption
- Seeds

Have you ever eaten black-eyed peas for New Year's? They are a traditional dish eaten for good luck on the holiday—especially in the South. Despite their common name, black-eyed peas are really a bean (in the legume family). Beans of different types are a major ingredient in dishes served all over the world. In their dried form, they can be stored for years and then soaked in water to bring back their soft texture. In this science activity, you will explore how the temperature of the water used to rehydrate dried black-eyed peas affects how quickly they become rehydrated—and ready to cook up!

BACKGROUND

Beans come in many shapes, sizes, and colors and have been eaten throughout the world for thousands of years. They are good sources of protein, carbohydrates, and fiber. The U.S. Department of Agriculture dietary guidelines suggest that beans, along with other foods that are low in fat, oils, and sugars (including vegetables and grains) should make up the largest part of our daily meals.

In addition to their nutritious qualities, beans are convenient because they can be dried and stored for years. Soaking the beans in water for a few hours (or less) softens the dried beans and prepares them for cooking. This rehydration process also occurs in nature. Beans are a form of seed, and they can sprout when exposed to water. Beans remain viable (able to grow) for long periods of time if they are kept dry, a feature that allows them to survive long periods of drought in natural settings—and one that allows us to store them for long periods of time prior to cooking. As beans soak in water, their volume increases. In this science activity, you will determine how soaking beans in hot versus cold water affects how quickly they absorb water.

MATERIALS

- Ice cubes
- Bowl
- Cold tap water
- Hot tap water
- 1 cup of dried black-eyed peas. Alternatively, dried split peas, lentils, or other legumes that do not need to soak long before cooking could be used.
- Two plastic, transparent disposable cups, at least 1.5 cups in size
- Measuring cup
- Permanent marker
- Timer or clock
- Ruler (optional)

PREPARATION

- Fill the bowl half full with ice cubes and then add cold tap water to the bowl, nearly filling it. You will use this as a source of ice water.
- Fill each plastic cup with 1/2 cup of dried black-eyed peas. Gently shake each cup so that the beans flatten out on the surface.
- Use a permanent marker to make a line on the side of each cup, lining up with the top of the black-eyed peas. You will want to have the cups on the edge of a counter (or table) and look straight-on at the top of the beans to make this mark correctly. *How do you think the bean level will change when water is added to the cups?*

PROCEDURE

- At the same time, fill one plastic cup with ice-cold water (from the bowl of ice cubes and water you prepared, being careful to not add any frozen bits of ice) and fill the other cup with very hot tap water. Fill both cups to the top with water.
- Set a timer, or note what time it is, and check on the cups every 10 minutes for the next 45 minutes. When you check on them, make a small line on each cup where the top of the beans are. Write the time next to the mark. *How does the bean level in each cup change over time?*
- *After 45 minutes (or longer), which cup has the higher bean level? What does this tell you about whether cold or hot water is more quickly absorbed by the beans?*

SCIENCE FAIR IDEA

Another way to measure your results in this activity is to weigh the black-eyed peas with a scale. You could use multiple cups and weigh the beans from those cups (after straining out the water) as they are soaked in water for various lengths of time (such as 30 minutes or one hour). *How does the mass of the black-eyed peas change over time? Is there an amount of time after which the beans remain roughly the same weight?*

SCIENCE FAIR IDEA

Try this activity using various types of legumes (legumes include beans, peas, and lentils). *Do some legumes absorb water faster than others? What does this tell you about how long they might need to be soaked before cooking them?*

OBSERVATIONS AND RESULTS

Did you find that the black-eyed peas had a higher level in the cup with the hot water over time compared to in the cup with the ice-cold water?

When dried beans are soaked in water, their volume increases as they absorb the water. Beans absorb hot water more quickly than cold water, which is why the black-eyed peas used in this activity should have swelled faster in the hot water than in the cold water. For example, after only 10 minutes of soaking, you may have seen that the level of the black-eyed peas in the hot water cup was about half an inch (1.3 cm) higher than the level in the cold water cup, and that this difference remained consistent for the rest of the activity. This activity works well for dried black-eyed peas, split peas, and lentils because they do not require much soaking before cooking; if you were to test other legumes that require more soaking, you would see that they absorb water much more slowly.

CLEANUP

When you are done with this activity, you could discard the beans—or you could include them in a bean-based recipe of your choice, such as black-eyed pea soup!

Sweet Science

Dancing Conversation Hearts

TAKE A CHANCE ON THIS VALENTINE'S DAY CHEMISTRY CHALLENGE!

PROJECT TIME

5-10 minutes

KEY CONCEPTS

Chemistry
Carbonation
Chemical reactions
Candy

Have you ever opened a fresh bottle of carbonated water or soda, poured a glass of it, and just watched as the bubbles fizzed upward in the glass? Have you ever wondered what those bubbles are? They're made of carbon dioxide gas, which was packed tight in the soda before you opened the bottle. Not only can that carbon dioxide gas give you a fizzy drink to enjoy, but it can also give you a show. How? By making candy conversation hearts "dance"! Along the way you will discover some of the fun chemistry for this entertaining activity. So this Valentine's Day if you receive some conversation hearts, you can grab a glass of soda and try out this science activity to explore another way to enjoy the candies—by watching them slowly dance!

BACKGROUND

A carbonated beverage, such as a bottle of soda, is packed full of dissolved carbon dioxide gas. But you don't see bubbles of carbon dioxide gas while the bottle is still sealed. Why is this? Soda in bottles (and cans) is prepared and kept in pressurized conditions that force the gas to stay blended into the liquid—in solution. As soon as the bottle or can is opened, however, the pressure is reduced, allowing some of the gas to escape from solution—and turn into fizzy carbon dioxide bubbles! Pouring the soda into a glass releases even more bubbles. But how can this process lead to dancing candy?

Conversation hearts—common gifts for Valentine's Day—are denser than soda, so if they're placed in a glass of soda, they will fall to the bottom. But what happens next? Try out this science activity to find out!

MATERIALS

- At least four conversation hearts
- A fresh bottle or can of colorless soda (unopened), such as Sprite or 7-Up
- A tall, clear glass

PREPARATION

- Get out your unopened soda, the glass, and four conversation hearts.
- Place everything in an area near a sink in case your soda overflows.

PROCEDURE

- Fill the glass nearly to the top with the fresh soda.
- Take the four conversation hearts and drop them, one at a time, into the soda. *What happens when you drop the hearts into the soda?*
- Watch the soda for a few seconds. *What happens to the conversation hearts shortly after they've been dropped into the soda?*
- Watch the soda for at least five minutes more. *What happens to the conversation hearts in the soda over time?*
- *Can you explain the behavior of the conversation hearts in the soda? How do you think carbon dioxide gas is involved?*

EXTRA

Try this science activity again but this time use other candies. *Do you get the same results with other candies? If they do not "dance," why do you think this is?*

EXTRA

Instead of using soda, try using water with vinegar and baking soda, which will also create carbon dioxide gas. Specifically, try filling a glass about half full with water, mix in one teaspoon of baking soda, add the conversation hearts and then slowly add vinegar until the glass is nearly full. *Do the conversation hearts "dance" in the baking soda and vinegar mixture?*

OBSERVATIONS AND RESULTS

Did the conversation hearts first sink to the bottom of the glass but then, over time, float back up—and then down again—in the soda, "dancing"?

In this activity you dropped conversation hearts into a glass of freshly poured carbonated soda. Because the conversation hearts are denser than soda, they should have quickly fallen to the bottom of the glass. But then something interesting should have happened. After a couple of minutes, some (or all) of the four candies should have slowly begun to rise up through the soda. The carbon dioxide bubbles in the soda were sticking to the candies, and when enough lighter-than-soda bubbles accumulated on a given candy, they should have lifted it up through the soda. Once at the top of the soda the carbon dioxide bubbles could escape into the air, causing the candy to sink once again. But as the candy sank, more bubbles should have stuck to it, causing it to rise again and repeat the cycle. This up-and-down motion makes the conversation heart candies appear to slowly "dance" in the soda.

CLEANUP

When you're finished with this activity you may pour out the soda and throw away the conversation hearts—or enjoy them as a snack!

Saint Patrick's Day Science

Brew Up Some Green Soda Pop!

GET YOUR SAINT PATRICK'S DAY POPPING WITH A CARBONATED CHEMISTRY CHALLENGE!

Have you ever wondered how carbonated soda is made? As you sip it, the bubbles in soda tickle your tongue's taste buds and propel the ingredients to the top of your mouth and nose so that you get a kick of flavor. But how do the bubbles, fizz, and taste get into the water? In this tasty science activity you will work with baking soda, citric acid, and sugar to create your own soda! And after you develop your recipe, add a few drops of green food coloring and you've got a festive drink you could share with friends and family to celebrate Saint Patrick's Day!

PROJECT TIME

10–15 minutes

KEY CONCEPTS

Chemistry
Chemical reactions
Food science
Carbonation

BACKGROUND

Soda is basically carbonated water with sugar added. Water becomes carbonated when a gas called carbon dioxide (CO_2) has been dissolved into it under high pressure. When you open a can or bottle of soda, the pressure is released and the CO_2 starts to come out of the solution. The escaping gas is what causes the bubbles in the beverage. Carbonation also occurs in nature, when water underground comes in contact with a source of carbon, such as limestone. The high-pressure reaction underground between the water and limestone forces CO_2 to dissolve into the water. When the water eventually rises to Earth's surface, the pressure is released and bubbly water is the result.

In this science activity, instead of pressure, you'll use baking soda (also called sodium bicarbonate), citric acid, and sugar to develop your own recipe for a soda drink. When you mix baking soda and citric acid together with water, a chemical reaction takes place that creates CO_2, along with sodium citrate. (Sodium citrate, like the other compounds you'll be using in this activity, is a harmless substance that's safe to eat or drink.)

MATERIALS

- At least five cups
- Baking soda
- Citric acid (Look for it in the canning or baking section of a supermarket.)
- Sugar
- Water
- Green food coloring
- Spoon or fork for stirring
- Measuring spoons
- Measuring cup

PREPARATION

- Measure out and add 1/4 teaspoon of citric acid to three of your cups. Leave the other two cups empty.

PROCEDURE

- To one of the cups holding citric acid add 1/16 teaspoon baking soda. (Measure 1/16 teaspoon by filling a 1/8 teaspoon measuring spoon half full.)
- Add 1/4 cup (59 ml) of cool water to the cup with citric acid and baking soda in it, mixing them together with a spoon or fork. *Are there a lot of bubbles? Is the liquid mildly bubbly or is it bubbling a lot?*
- Taste a little bit of the beverage. *How does it feel on your tongue? Is it too gritty? Do you find the feeling of the liquid in your mouth pleasant?*
- After tasting the beverage feel free to spit out the liquid (into one of the empty cups). It will not harm you to swallow it, but it might not taste very much like soda yet, and you also don't want to over-acidify your stomach (which could give you a slight stomachache) because there is still more taste testing to do.
- To one of the two remaining cups with citric acid, add and mix together 1/4 teaspoon baking soda and 1/4 cup (59 ml) of cool water. *Are there more or less bubbles with this mixture?*
- Again taste a little bit of the beverage. *How does it feel on your tongue? Is it gritty or do you find the feeling to be pleasant?* Again, you can spit out the liquid into an empty cup after tasting it.
- To the last cup with citric acid in it add and mix together 1 teaspoon baking soda and 1/4 cup (59 ml) of cool water. *Are there more or less bubbles with this mixture?*
- Again, taste some of the beverage. *How does it feel on your tongue? Is it gritty or pleasant?* As with the other samples, you should spit it out afterward.
- Decide which recipe you enjoyed the best. Make up a fresh 1/4 cup (59 ml) of it (the same way you made it before). Then mix in 1/4 teaspoon of sugar. *How does it taste? Does it taste like a soda pop?*

- Continue to mix in 1/4 teaspoon of sugar at a time, tasting it after you add the sugar each time and keeping track of how much you have added. (Add no more than 1 teaspoon sugar total.) *What amount of added sugar makes for the tastiest soda pop?*
- After you've decided how much sugar to add to your baking soda and citric acid mixture, you can scale up the recipe to make a festive, green-colored beverage! For example, if you found that 1/4 teaspoon of baking soda and 1/4 teaspoon of sugar worked well in 1/4 cup (59 ml) of water, you could make 1 cup (236 ml) of soda with 1 cup (236 ml) of water, 1 teaspoon of baking soda, 1 teaspoon of sugar, and 1 teaspoon of citric acid. Then, mix in just three drops of green food coloring, and your festive beverage is ready to share and enjoy!

EXTRA

Ask your friends and family to taste the final recipe that you developed. *Do they enjoy the beverage as much as you do?* Collect their feedback and see if you can develop a recipe that everyone enjoys. You could also try adding flavorings such as vanilla, cinnamon, or a little bit of crushed fruit.

EXTRA

Do this activity again but test a wider variety of baking soda and citric acid recipes (such as including the 1/8 teaspoon and 1/2 teaspoon baking soda recipes). Then try to numerically rank (such as on a scale of 1 to 5) how gritty and bubbly each combination is. *Which recipe makes the bubbliest soda pop? What about the least gritty one? Overall, which recipe do you like the best?*

EXTRA

Some fruits contain citric acid. Try re-creating your soda recipe using juice from a fruit that contains citric acid—such as a lemon or a lime—instead of using food-grade citric acid. *How does the amount of fruit juice compare with the quantity of food-grade citric acid in your ideal flavor combination?*

OBSERVATIONS AND RESULTS

Was the recipe that used 1/4 teaspoon of baking soda and 1/2 teaspoon of sugar the best, tasting the most like a normal soda pop?

In this activity, when you combined baking soda and citric acid (with water), the chemical reaction should have made fizzy CO_2 bubbles, making all of the recipes you tested produce at least some bubbles. The recipe with the least amount of baking soda added (1/16 teaspoon) should have made the fewest, shortest-lived bubbles whereas the recipe with the most baking soda (1 teaspoon) should have been clearly the fizziest. This is because there is more baking soda available to react with the citric acid, making CO_2 bubbles. The recipe with 1 teaspoon of baking soda, however, was likely rather gritty and bitter, due to the large amount of baking soda. This probably made the recipe using 1/4 teaspoon baking soda the ideal recipe in terms of bubbliness, flavor, and texture. You may also have found that adding 1/2 teaspoon of sugar was the ideal amount, but this can vary based on personal preference.

CLEANUP

After this activity, dispose of any beverages you didn't drink. Put away the ingredients and wash your measuring cups and spoons.

Silky Science Tie-Dyeing Eggs

MAKE EASTER MORE COLORFUL WITH THIS EASTER EGG CHEMISTRY CHALLENGE!

Have you ever dyed eggs? Turning eggshells from white into different, dazzling colors can be a lot of fun! Many people do this around Easter time using dye tablets to make different colors in liquid form. They then dip the egg into the liquid and wait until it turns the desired color. Eggs can be dyed in many other ways, and one neat method uses silk ties. Sounds strange to use clothing to dye eggs, right? But it actually works really well! In this activity you'll dye eggs with silk ties and investigate whether heat is needed for the process to work well. Aren't you just dyeing to try this out?

PROJECT TIME

45 minutes

KEY CONCEPTS

Chemistry
Dyes
Dyeing eggs
Chemical reactions

BACKGROUND

People have been dyeing eggs long before the common store-bought tablet coloring existed. Over the years people have explored many other ways to do it, such as by using dyes from plants and spices or by using completely different methods. One way you can dye eggs is using old, 100 percent silk neckties. To dye an egg using silk ties, the egg is wrapped in the tie, and they are placed in water with vinegar. When the process is done, some of the dye from the tie transfers to the eggshell. Ideally, it dyes the eggshell so that it looks similar to the tie, with some detailed designs being clearly visible on the eggshell.

Silk is usually dyed using a specific group of dyes known as acid dyes, which color objects by chemically reacting with proteins in them (such as the silk fibers in the ties with eggshell proteins). For the chemical reaction to work (that is, change an object's color), this type of dye needs acids around. Thus, the eggs are soaked with vinegar (an acid) during the dyeing process to help the acid dyes transfer their color from the silk ties to the eggshells.

MATERIALS

- All-silk necktie. Look at the tags on the back of the tie to make sure it is 100 percent. Darker blues, purples, and reds transfer dye the best. These ties can usually be purchased inexpensively at a secondhand shop or thrift store. (Be sure to ask permission before using someone's silk tie for this activity—the ties will be destroyed in the process of dyeing!)
- Scissors
- Two raw white eggs
- Four twist ties
- Light-colored tablecloth, pillowcase, or other light-weight, light-colored fabric scrap. Use fabric that you will not mind having cut up.
- Cooking pot
- Large bowl or another cooking pot, similar in size to the first cooking pot
- Measuring cups
- Water
- White vinegar

- Well-ventilated stove area, such as provided by an overhead ventilation system or a nearby window that could be opened, or dust masks.
- Timer or clock
- Old dishtowels or rags
- Tongs or slotted spoon
- Vegetable oil (optional)

PREPARATION

- Take the silk tie and turn it over so that you are looking at its back. Using scissors, have an adult help you carefully cut through the stitches going up the middle back of the tie. Open the tie up as you go. Remove any labels. Continue until you have cut through all of the stitches along the seam.

- Remove any (usually white) liners running along the inside of the tie. If there is a liner sewed to the bottom of the tie, carefully cut along the seams to remove this liner. Try to only cut the liner part of the tie.

- Flip the tie over so that its front is facing up. *What colors are on the tie and does it have any patterns/designs? How do you think this will dye the eggs?* Place an egg a few inches away from the tip of the tie and fold the tie's tip over the egg so that it completely covers the egg. Adjust the position of the egg in the tie so that you can gather up enough tie material on one end to bind the material together.

- Once you are satisfied with the egg's position, cut off the piece of tie in which the egg is wrapped. Cut straight across the width of the tie.

- Pinch the tie material around the egg so that it is tight, but be careful not to break the egg! Twist a twist tie around the fabric at the end of the egg. To smooth all of the wrinkles, carefully pull the fabric through the twist tie to tighten it around the egg.

- Take a new egg and place it on the tie several inches above where you just cut the tie. Wrap this egg in a higher-up piece of the tie material as you did with the first egg.
- Wrap each egg in a second layer of lightweight, light-colored fabric scrap to help hold the piece of tie next to the egg. *Why do you think it's important that the fabric be light-colored?* For each egg, cut the fabric so that you have enough to cover the egg, wrap the new fabric around the egg, twist a twist tie around the end of the egg (on top of the other twist tie), and tighten the light-colored fabric as you did with the tie material.
- Adult supervision is required when using the stove. A dust mask or a well-ventilated stove area is needed to avoid breathing in vinegar and dye fumes. Some acid dyes are toxic whereas others are nontoxic. Without knowing exactly which acid dyes are in the ties you will be using, it is best to practice caution and avoid breathing in possibly dangerous dye fumes when heating the ties in hot water. Do not eat the eggs!

PROCEDURE

- Place one of the wrapped eggs in a cooking pot. This egg will be boiled. Place the other wrapped egg, which will not be boiled, in a similar-size large bowl or pot. *How well do you think the boiled egg will be dyed compared to the non-boiled egg?*
- Use a measuring cup to add water to the pot until there is at least about 1 inch (2.5 cm) of water above the egg. Add the same amount of water to the egg in the bowl.
- Add 1/4 cup (59 ml) of white vinegar to each egg. *Why is adding vinegar important?*

- Place the pot with the egg to be boiled onto the stove. Have an adult turn the burner on to medium-high and cover the pot with a lid. To avoid inhaling the vinegar and possibly dangerous dye fumes, leave the lid on the pot while its on the stove, turn on an overhead stove fan and/or open a nearby window or put on a dust mask (and have anyone in the kitchen area put on a dust mask as well). It is also recommended to stay out of the kitchen for the most part during the boiling process.
- Leave the other wrapped egg remaining in its bowl on a counter.
- With an adult's help, check on the pot on the stove every few minutes to see if the water's boiling. After it comes to a boil have an adult remove the lid and reduce heat to medium so that the water is simmering. Let the egg simmer for 20 minutes.
- After simmering, have an adult use tongs or a slotted spoon to carefully remove the egg from the water and place it on some old dish towels or rags on the counter. Also remove the egg that was not boiled and place it on the old dish towels. Keep track of which egg is which.
- Let the eggs sit on the dish towels until they are both cool enough to unwrap. This should take about 10 minutes.
- Carefully unwrap the eggs (undoing the twist ties and removing the fabric layers).
- Compare the eggs. *How does the egg that was boiled look compared with the egg that was not? Which egg looks like it dyed better, or darker? How do you think heating the egg affected the chemical reaction that took place between the acid dyes (in the tie material) and the eggshell? Do you think heating the egg helped the chemical reaction to work better?*
- If you like, rub the eggs with a little vegetable oil to make them shiny.

EXTRA

It is possible to use the same tie to dye eggs multiple times. Try doing this to see how well it works. *How many times can you dye an egg using the same piece of tie so that the colors from the silk tie still transfer to the eggshell with the same darkness and details? Do some colors last longer than others?*

SCIENCE FAIR IDEA

In this activity you put the eggs in a certain amount of water with 1/4 cup (59 ml) of white vinegar. Try repeating this activity keeping all of the conditions the same but changing the ratio of water to vinegar. For example, if you used 5 cups (1.2 l) of water and 1/4 cup (59 ml) of vinegar, you could also try 5 1/4 cups (1.25 l) of water and no vinegar as well as 4 3/4 cups (1.1 l) water and 1/2 cup (118 ml) vinegar. *Do the eggs dye better using more or less vinegar? Do they dye at all when you add no vinegar?*

SCIENCE FAIR IDEA

Vinegar is a mild acid that you used in this activity because acid dyes are commonly used to dye silk. *Do you think other acids, or even bases, could be used to dye the eggshells using silk ties?* You could learn more about acids, bases, and the pH scale, make a hypothesis about how well you think different acids and/or bases will dye the eggs, and then repeat this activity to test your hypothesis. Be sure always to find out and follow the necessary safety precautions for using different chemicals and to always ask for adult supervision when using them.

OBSERVATIONS AND RESULTS

Did the boiled egg dye much better, or more darkly, than the non-boiled egg?

For the acid dyes to color the eggshell (or silk fibers in the tie), they must undergo a chemical reaction that forms a chemical bond between the dye and the eggshell proteins (or silk fibers in the tie). As mentioned earlier, acid (for example, vinegar) is needed to help this reaction work well. (Acid specifically makes chemical groups on the proteins become positively charged so they can react with the negatively charged dye molecules.) In addition to acid, this chemical reaction also needs heat to work well. To effectively dye silk fibers using acid dyes, a great deal of heat is necessary. Similarly, you should have seen that the boiled egg was dyed much better (or more darkly) than the non-boiled egg. If you used a light-colored tie, the boiled egg may have been visibly dyed whereas the non-boiled egg remained white. If you used a dark-colored tie, the boiled egg should have been darkly dyed and the non-boiled egg may have taken on some very light, faded coloring as well.

CLEANUP

You can store the eggs temporarily in the refrigerator. Do not eat any of the eggs you used in this activity because clothing dyes used in ties are not made to be safe to eat. The eggs that were boiled will be hard-boiled, but the eggs that were not boiled will still be raw. Wash your hands after handling them.

Sudsy Science

Creating Homemade Bath Bombs

MAKE A BOMB MOTHER'S DAY TREAT USING SCIENCE!

PROJECT TIME

1 Hour to 1 Day

KEY CONCEPTS

Chemistry
Chemical reaction
Acids
Bases
Water

Have you ever had a refreshing bath with bubbles or bath salts? What if you could use chemistry to create a bath-time treat that combined both fizzing bubbles and soothing salts? Such a combination does exist, and it's called a bath bomb. If you have never experienced one, these "bombs" become fizzy when they touch the water. Why? It is due to a chemical reaction taking place between different ingredients within the bath bomb. In this activity, you'll get to make your own homemade bath bombs and explore how changing the ratio of the ingredients affects how much the bath bomb fizzes when it comes into contact with water. Then you can use your perfected method to make some bath bombs as a gift for Mother's Day!

BACKGROUND

Bath bombs can have a wide range of ingredients, including bath salts (which can help soothe muscles), food coloring, fragrances, and other components. There are, however, a few key ingredients that most homemade recipes have: baking soda and citric acid. Why is this? When baking soda and citric acid are mixed and are then put in water, they undergo a chemical reaction. The reaction produces lots of bubbles, which you see as the bath bomb dissolves in the water. These bubbles that make the water become so fizzy are made of carbon dioxide gas.

Another ingredient that is often used in homemade bath bombs is cornstarch. This ingredient can act as a dry "filler" that gets mixed in with the reactive baking soda and citric acid in the bath bombs. In this activity you'll explore how changing the amount of cornstarch filler affects how fizzy the bath bombs turn out and you'll figure out what goes into making the most impressive bath bomb.

MATERIALS

- Citric acid (This is usually available at grocery stores in the canning section.)
- Baking soda
- Cornstarch
- Water
- Measuring spoons
- Vegetable oil
- Food coloring (at least two different colors)
- Medicine dropper
- Forks and spoons for mixing
- Optional ingredients to add to your bath bombs: Epsom salts and fragrance (such as essential oils).
- Four bowls
- A muffin tray or ice cube tray (If you are using a muffin tray, you can dry the bath bombs for 45 minutes in an oven or overnight at room temperature. If you live in a very humid environment, it's recommended to oven dry the bath bombs. If you use an ice cube tray, however, you can only dry the bath bombs overnight at room temperature.)
- A bathtub to make a hot bath and test your bath bombs in

PREPARATION

- If you are using a muffin tray, preheat the oven to 170°F (76.6°C) (or its lowest setting). Always have an adult help when using the oven.

- Note that the recipe amounts given in this activity are for approximately filling one muffin cup, or about three ice cube cups, but this greatly depends on the exact size of the cups in your muffin or ice cube tray. If you want to make additional bath bombs, you can double or triple the recipes.

PROCEDURE

- In one bowl mix 1 1/3 tablespoons of citric acid, 2 2/3 tablespoons of baking soda, and 2 tablespoons of cornstarch. If you are using Epsom salts, you can also add 2 teaspoons to the mix.

- In a second bowl mix 1 teaspoon of vegetable oil, 1 teaspoon of water, and two drops of food coloring. If you want to include fragrance, also add 15 drops into the mixture. Be sure to rinse and clean the medicine dropper and measuring spoons in between measuring the different ingredients.

- Using a clean medicine dropper, add a few drops of the wet mixture to the dry ingredients in the first bowl. *What happens when you add a drop of the wet mixture?* You should see it fizz—this is the bath bomb reaction taking place! Because you don't want the bath bombs to react yet, quickly press down on the fizzy spot with the back of a clean spoon. This should stop the fizziness. Mix in the damp spot with the rest of the ingredients in the bowl. Repeat this process until you have added, and thoroughly mixed in, all of the wet ingredients (a few drops at a time) to the dry ingredients.

- **Tip:** Part of the challenge of making homemade bath bombs is adding the right amount of wet ingredients. If you live in a humid environment, you may not need to add all of the wet ingredients. If the bath bomb mixture appears to continue to puff up even after you have thoroughly mixed in some wet ingredients, then the mixture may be too wet. If this happens, start over making the bath bombs from the beginning, but this time use less water in the recipe. If you find that this first recipe works better using less water, adjust the following bath bomb recipe similarly.

- Use a clean medicine dropper to drop one drop of vegetable oil into each cup on the tray that you will be using. Then use a finger to spread the oil all around each cup's surface.

- Fill one of the tray's cups with the bath bomb mixture. Add a spoonful at a time and use the back of the spoon and/or the palm of your hand to press the mixture down into the cup continually as the mixture is added to the cup. If you are filling multiple cups, evenly divide up the mixture between them.

- In a third bowl, combine 1 tablespoon of citric acid, 2 tablespoons of baking soda, and 3 tablespoons of cornstarch. If you are using Epsom salts, add in 2 teaspoons.

- In a fourth bowl mix 1 teaspoon of vegetable oil, 2 1/2 teaspoons of water, and two drops of a different food coloring. If you want to include fragrance, also add 15 drops. Be sure to rinse and clean the medicine dropper and measuring spoons in between measuring the different ingredients.

- Use a clean medicine dropper to slowly mix the wet mixture with the dry ingredients in the third bowl, one drop at a time, as you did before, using the spoon to press down on fizzy spots and continually stir the mixture. Fill the tray's cups as similarly as possible to how you filled them for the first bath bomb recipe.

- Let the bath bombs dry. If you are using a muffin tray, dry the bombs overnight or turn off the oven (which was preheated to

170°F [76.6°C]) and let them stay in the (turned off) oven for 45 minutes with the oven door closed. If you are using a plastic ice cube tray, dry the bath bombs overnight at room temperature. Once the bath bombs have dried, carefully remove them from the cups.

- **Tip:** If the bath bombs are very crumbly, the recipes may not have had enough water in them. To fix this, you can remake the bath bombs but try using a little more water.
- Get ready to toss the bath bombs into a bath! Fill a tub with hot (but not scalding) bathwater. Then place the bath bombs in the tub. *What happens when the bath bombs are placed in the water? Is a bath bomb made from one recipe fizzier than a bath bomb made from the other recipe? Does one take longer to dissolve than the other one? Which do you think worked best? How do you think the amount of cornstarch in the recipes is related to your results?*

SCIENCE FAIR IDEA

In this activity you tested your bath bombs in hot bathwater, but they might behave differently in colder water. You could use a stopwatch or timer to see how long they take to dissolve in hot water and then compare it with placing them in cold water.

SCIENCE FAIR IDEA

Instead of citric acid, you could experiment with making bath bombs using citric acid substitutes, such as cream of tartar or lemon juice. *How do bath bombs made using a citric acid substitute compare with those made using citric acid?*

SCIENCE FAIR IDEA

In this activity you tried varying the amount of cornstarch but you could try making bath bombs without any cornstarch. *If bath bombs are made that don't have cornstarch, how do they compare with those made with cornstarch? Are they very different?*

OBSERVATIONS AND RESULTS

Did the bath bomb made using more cornstarch (following the second recipe) take longer to dissolve than the one made with less cornstarch (following the first recipe)? Did the one made with less cornstarch fizz more?

When a bath bomb comes in contact with water, the baking soda and citric acid react to make carbon dioxide bubbles. This is an acid-base reaction, where baking soda (also called sodium bicarbonate) is a weak base and citric acid is a weak acid. The cornstarch acts as a "filler" to control the reaction between the baking soda and citric acid. In this activity the second recipe used more cornstarch, and less baking soda and citric acid, compared with the first recipe. Consequently, you should have seen that a bath bomb made using the first recipe produced more vigorous bubbles and impressive fizzing, and dissolved much faster, compared with a bath bomb made using the second recipe. (The size of the bath bombs also affects how long it takes them to dissolve, because larger bath bombs will typically take longer than smaller ones to dissolve. But because the bombs from the different recipes should have been similar in size, this factor should not have greatly affected the comparison.)

CLEANUP

If you have extra bath bombs and want to save them for later, put them in a sealable plastic bag. Once you've settled on your favorite recipe, you can also make them and give them out as gifts!

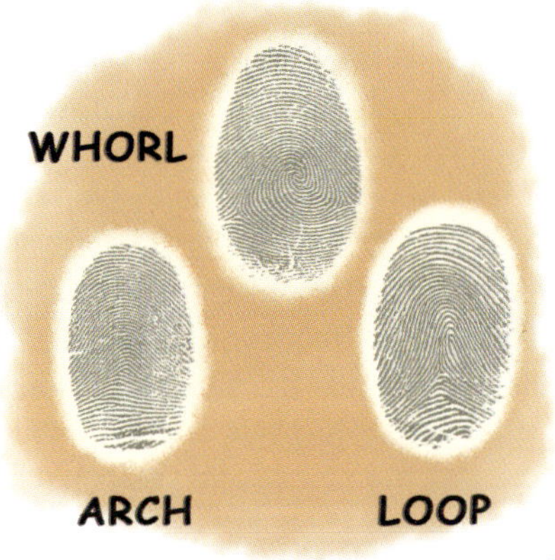

Succession Science

Are Fingerprint Patterns Inherited?

FIND OUT MORE ABOUT FINGERPRINTS IN A FATHER'S DAY INHERITANCE INVESTIGATION!

PROJECT TIME

10-15 minutes

KEY CONCEPTS

Genetics
Inheritance
Biology
Development
DNA

Have you ever seen a child who looked just like his or her father when the latter was younger? We can often tell that two people are related because they have several similar physical traits, such as facial features or hair color. This is because children receive half of their DNA (genetic blueprints) from each parent. But what about something small, such as fingerprints—are they an inherited trait? Fingerprints are used to identify people because each person's fingerprints are unique, but people can have similar fingerprint patterns. This Father's Day you could do this activity with your family to investigate whether fingerprint patterns are random or influenced by genetics. You'll be able to see if your fingerprint pattern is just one more trait that you can thank your father (and mother) for giving you.

BACKGROUND

You started getting your own unique fingerprints even before you were born! During weeks 10 through 24 of development, ridges form on the epidermis (outermost skin layer) of a fetus's fingertips. The patterns that these ridges make on each finger and thumb are known as fingerprints, which are static and do not change with age—so an individual will have the same fingerprints from infancy to adulthood. The patterns change size, but not shape, as the person grows. (To get a better idea of how that works, you can model the change in size by inking your fingerprint onto a balloon and then blowing up the balloon.) Because each person has unique fingerprints that do not change over time, these prints can be used for identification. For example, police use fingerprints to determine whether a particular individual has been at a crime scene.

Although the exact number, shape, and spacing of the ridges changes from person to person, fingerprints can be sorted into three general categories based on their pattern type: loop, arch, and whorl.

MATERIALS

- At least one pair of parents and their genetic son(s) or daughter(s) (The more members of the nuclear family that are available, the better the results will be.)
- Magnifying glass (optional)

PREPARATION

- Look at some drawings or pictures of the three basic fingerprint pattern types: loop, arch, and whorl. In a loop pattern, the ridges enter from either side, curve up and then exit usually from the same side they entered. In a whorl pattern, the ridges are usually circular. In an arch pattern the ridges enter from one side, make a small rise in the center, and exit generally on the opposite side.

- Become familiar with what the different types look like so you can readily identify them. Note that there is some variation on these basic types, such as the "tented arch," which looks like a more sharply curved version of the typical arch.

PROCEDURE

- Gather family members together so that you can look at their fingerprints as a group.
- One at a time, look at each person's right index finger where their fingerprint is. By looking at the pattern on the finger, characterize the pattern as a whorl, arch, or loop. You could use a magnifying glass to look at their finger more closely. *What type of fingerprint pattern do they have?*
- Look at the fingerprint pattern of other family members, one at a time, and characterize each as one of the three basic patterns. *What type of fingerprint patterns do other family members have? Do you see any trends?*
- *Overall, does it look like fingerprint patterns are inherited? In other words, did siblings usually have the same fingerprint pattern and did people have fingerprint patterns in common with their parents?*

SCIENCE FAIR IDEA

Try this activity again but this time collect fingerprint pattern information from a lot more people to draw a better conclusion about whether fingerprint patterns are inherited. Try to get at least 15 related pairs of people (such as siblings) and at least 15 unrelated pairs of people. Compare the percentage of times that the pairs had matching fingerprint patterns. *Are the percentages the same for related and unrelated pairs? Which is higher? What does this tell you about whether fingerprint patterns are genetic?*

EXTRA

Try this activity with more people (related and/or unrelated). *Are some fingerprint patterns more common than others?*

EXTRA

Toes also have ridge patterns. *Do "toe prints" follow the same rules as fingerprints?*

OBSERVATIONS AND RESULTS

Did you see some examples of fingerprint patterns being inherited?

There is an inheritance component to fingerprint patterns but the genetics of how they are inherited are complicated. (Multiple genes are involved.) Fingerprints are also affected by a person's environment while developing in the womb. Because of this, you may have seen some examples of fingerprint patterns likely being inherited (such as a son and/or daughter having the same pattern type as their father). But this may not have always been the case for individuals you know to be closely related. To more clearly see how fingerprint patterns are inherited, you would need to use a much larger sample size, such as described in the Science Fair Idea box. Because each person's fingerprints are unique, and not even identical twins—who share the same DNA—have identical fingerprints, this also shows that fingerprints are not completely controlled by genetics.

CLEANUP

After you've completed this activity, simply put away your magnifying glass and thank your family.

Sizzling Science

Exploring the Chemistry of Fireworks

GET FIRED UP FOR AN INDEPENDENCE DAY SCIENCE DEMONSTRATION!

PROJECT TIME

15 minutes

KEY CONCEPTS

Chemicals
Metals
Fire
Atoms
Energy

Have you ever watched a firework show and wondered how all the different colors—amazing reds, yellows, blues, purples, greens and more—are made? The color, or colors, that a firework makes depends on what color-producing chemicals are in it. These chemicals are various metals that burn when the firework goes off, and it's the burning metals that create the bright colors. Different metals give off different, specific colors. In this science activity, you will get to burn some metals at home to investigate what colors they make. Then at the next fireworks show, you can impress friends and family with your knowledge of what may be causing some of the colors they see!

BACKGROUND

Astronomers can figure out what distant stars are made of (in other words, their atomic composition) by seeing what type of light the star produces. In this activity you will do something similar by observing the color of flames when various chemicals are burned. How does it work exactly? It comes down to atoms and energy.

All matter is made of atoms. Atoms have a nucleus that is surrounded by electrons. Electrons moving around the nucleus have certain amounts of energy, called energy levels. If electrons gain energy, they move from their energy level to a higher one through distinct steps. Likewise, if electrons lose energy, they drop to a lower energy level. The lost energy can be carried away in the form of heat or as light (a photon). Exactly how much energy is lost affects what kind of light is made, which we may see as a difference in its color.

MATERIALS

- Adult helper
- Table salt (chemical name: sodium chloride)
- Small plastic bag
- Six bamboo skewers
- White glue
- Copper sulfate (This is available via pet or aquarium stores and is used to combat algae or it is sold by home improvement stores as a root killer. Make sure the product is pure copper sulfate and that it is in the form of powder or small crystals.)
- Matches or lighter
- Candle (Choose one that can either stand on its own or has a sturdy stand.)
- Outdoor surface (A place where you can safely burn a candle after it becomes twilight or dark outside. Be sure it is in an open area to allow good airflow.)
- Container of water
- Disposable gloves (These are strongly recommended for handling the copper sulfate.)
- Safety goggles (recommended)
- Flashlight (optional)

PREPARATION

- Pour a small amount of table salt (roughly 1 tablespoon) into a small plastic bag.
- Apply a thin layer of glue to the top 1 inch (2.5 cm) of the tip of a skewer. Just a little bit of glue is enough.
- Dip the glue-coated tip of the skewer into the salt in the bag. Twist the skewer back and forth a bit to coat the skewer's tip with the salt. Set the skewer aside to dry. Repeat this with two more skewers so you have a total of three skewers that have their tips coated with salt.
- Next, have an adult coat three more skewers with copper sulfate. Read and follow all safety precautions on the packaging that the copper sulfate came in. Be careful not to let anybody inhale any copper sulfate dust or get any on their skin or face. If desired, use disposable gloves and safety goggles. If not using gloves, be sure not to touch the copper sulfate. Coat the last inch (2.5 cm) of the tip of a skewer in a thin layer of glue and dip the glue-coated tip into the bag of blue-colored copper sulfate, twisting it back and forth to coat the tip. Repeat this with two more skewers so that you have three with coated tips.
- Allow all six of your skewers to dry. This may take about half an hour.
- When you later burn the skewers, be sure to do it in an open, outdoor area and be careful not to breathe the fumes or smoke from the skewers coated in copper sulfate.
- Adult supervision is required when using fire, burning the skewers and handling the copper sulfate.

PROCEDURE

- When it is dark (or twilight), take your candle, matches, and prepared skewers to an open area outside where you can safely burn a candle. Be sure there is good airflow and always stand upwind of the flame (so that the breeze carries the smoke away from you). Also have a container of water with you as a safety precaution.
- Have an adult light the candle.
- Once the candle is burning well and you are on the upwind side of the flame, carefully take out one of the prepared skewers and hold the chemical-coated end in the flame. Be sure not to breathe the fumes or smoke from the burning skewer! *What color does the chemical burn? How does it compare with the normal color of the candle's flame?* You may be able to see the color in the candle's flame or by holding the skewer away from the candle (once the chemicals have caught fire) and looking at the flame on the tip of the skewer.
- The skewer may also catch fire after a few moments. If this happens, remove it from the flame and extinguish it in the container of water.
- Repeat this process for the other five skewers. (To help you distinguish which chemical you are burning, remember that the skewers coated in sodium chloride [table salt] will have white-coated tips and those coated in copper sulfate will have blue-coated ones.) *Which color does the sodium chloride burn? Which color does the copper sulfate burn?*

EXTRA

You could try this activity using other metals known to produce certain flame colors when burned. Be sure to always look into and follow all proper safety precautions when handling different chemicals and burning them. *What colors do other metals make when burned?*

OBSERVATIONS AND RESULTS

Did the sodium chloride-coated tip burn pure yellow-orange and the copper sulfate burn bluish-green?

A typical flame will burn yellow-orange with a little bit of blue near the base of the wick. When you burned the skewer tip coated with sodium chloride, you should have seen that the flame was pure yellow-orange (without any blue). This is because when the metal sodium is burned, it makes intense yellow-orange light. When you burned the skewer tip coated with copper sulfate, you should have seen that the flame gained blue-green traces. This is because when the metal copper is burned, it makes bluish-green light.

If an atom's electrons lose energy, they drop down to a lower energy level, and the lost energy can be released as light. Different types of atoms, or elements, have different gaps between their energy levels, which causes them to make light of different colors when they're burned and lose that energy.

CLEANUP

Be sure to extinguish (put out) the candle and the skewers when you are done with the activity. When you are sure they have been extinguished (after dipping them in the water container), you can dispose of the used skewers in the garbage.

Shining Science

Explore Glow-in-the-Dark Water!

LET'S DO A CHEMISTRY CHALLENGE AND GET READY TO GLOW!

Have you ever wondered how glow-in-the-dark things work? It can be a lot of fun to play with bracelets, wands, and other toys that are glow-in-the-dark! Did you ever imagine that you could make something at home that glows? It turns out that it's not that hard to do—all you need is tonic water and a black light! Some common household chemicals can also affect this beverage's glow. In this activity, you'll make tonic water glow by using a black light, and then you'll add a little bleach to the water. How will adding bleach affect the tonic water's glow? Try this activity to find out!

PROJECT TIME

10-15 minutes

KEY CONCEPTS

Chemistry
Water
Light
Fluorescence
Energy
Ultraviolet light

BACKGROUND

Tonic water is a carbonated beverage that has a chemical called quinine dissolved in it. Quinine is made from the bark of a tree and has been used for centuries as a treatment for malaria. Quinine not only gives tonic water a characteristic bitter taste (which is offset today by the addition of sweeteners to bottled tonic water) but this chemical can also be very fluorescent under the right conditions.

Under an ultraviolet "black light," the quinine in tonic water makes the water fluoresce a brilliant, bright blue (even though only a relatively small amount of quinine is dissolved in the water). In general, something fluoresces because it has absorbed light energy, which makes it excited, and then it releases (or emits) light as it returns to its normal, unexcited state. Part of why we find things that glow under ultraviolet lights—such as some minerals, fish, and tonic water—to be fascinating is because we cannot see the (ultraviolet) light they absorb but can see the visible light they emit (which is blue in the case of quinine).

MATERIALS

- Tonic water
- Clear plastic disposable cup
- Measuring cup (optional)
- Medicine dropper
- Bleach
- Ultraviolet "black light" bulb (This can be purchased at a party supply store or some hardware stores.)
- A room that can be darkened

PREPARATION

- When handling the bleach, be sure to read and follow all safety precautions listed on the container. Adult assistance is required when handling bleach. Do not drink the bleach or the tonic water mixed with the bleach, and be careful to not get it on your skin.

- Avoid looking directly at the ultraviolet "black light" and shining it on your skin because the light can damage your eyes and skin.

PROCEDURE

- Pour about 1 cup (236 ml) of tonic water into a clear plastic, disposable cup.
- In a darkened room, turn on the ultraviolet black light and shine it on the cup. *What happens to the tonic water in the cup when the black light shines on it?*
- While still shining the black light on the cup of tonic water, use the medicine dropper to carefully add two drops of bleach to the tonic water. Carefully mix the bleach in with the tonic. *What happens when the bleach is added to the tonic? What happens after the bleach is mixed in with it?*
- If you do not see a change in the tonic water, try adding and mixing in a few more drops of bleach. *What happens?*
- If you have some left, under the black light you can compare the glow of the tonic water in the original bottle with the tonic water that has bleach mixed in. *Do they look very different? Overall, how did adding bleach to the tonic water change its glow under the black light?*

EXTRA

If you dilute tonic water with regular water, you can make the tonic water glow less brightly. *What is the smallest amount of tonic needed (as you dilute it with normal water) for it to still visibly glow under an ultraviolet black light?*

EXTRA

Bleach is a type of chemical called an oxidizing agent. Some other common household oxidizing agents include hydrogen peroxide and OxiClean (which contains sodium percarbonate). *When other oxidizing agents are added to tonic water, do they have the same effect on its glow under an ultraviolet black light that bleach does?*

EXTRA

You could try preparing JELL-O with tonic water instead of regular water. *Does the JELL-O made with tonic water glow under an ultraviolet black light?* (Tip: Try preparing the JELL-O with water that is hot but not quite boiling.)

OBSERVATIONS AND RESULTS

When you added a few drops of bleach to the tonic water, did it stop fluorescing under the ultraviolet black light?

You should have clearly seen that the tonic water glowed a brilliant, bright blue color when you put it under the ultraviolet black light (before adding bleach). This is because the (invisible) ultraviolet light from the black light is absorbed by the quinine in the tonic water, and this excites the quinine. When the quinine becomes unexcited, it releases visible blue light that we see. After adding and mixing in a few drops of bleach with the tonic water, however, it should have stopped glowing. Why? Bleach is an oxidizing agent and can disrupt and break certain chemical bonds (specifically carbon-carbon double bonds). It is in these chemical bonds that the quinine absorbs the ultraviolet light, so by adding bleach to the tonic water it makes the quinine unable to absorb ultraviolet light anymore, and so it can no longer emit blue light.

CLEANUP

You can pour the very diluted bleach down a drain. Thoroughly clean anything that came in contact with the bleach and rinse your hands.

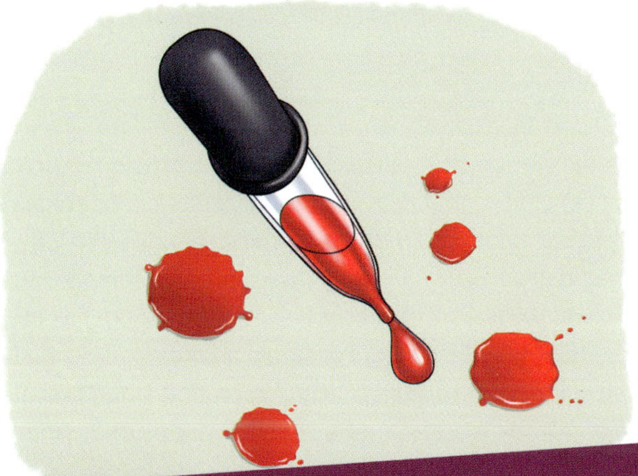

Crime Scene Science

Solve Mysteries by Investigating Drops

HAVE A BLOODY GOOD TIME WITH THIS A HALLOWEEN-THEMED ACTIVITY.

PROJECT TIME

45 minutes

KEY CONCEPTS

Forensics
Liquids
Physics
Models

Do you enjoy watching crime mysteries or reading about investigations? Every criminal leaves behind evidence at the crime scene. The trick to catching the lawbreaker is collecting all the evidence and making sense of it. This is what a forensic expert does. In this Halloween-themed science activity, you'll be correlating the size of bloodstains to a distance traveled—but don't get too grossed out; you'll be doing it all with fake blood. If you like figuring out mysteries and you don't mind a little gore, roll up your sleeves and get ready to crack the case!

BACKGROUND

Forensic science is any science that is used in the courtroom or judicial system, and it is extremely important. The goal of a forensic scientist is to remain impartial and to study all the available evidence in order to determine the truth—which can often determine what happened in a crime case. Forensic science includes many areas of study such as engineering, pathology, and biology. For example, if an athlete were to die suddenly while playing a game, a forensic scientist with a specialty in pathology and biology would be called in to find out the cause.

In crime scenes where people are wounded, investigators apply principles of liquid analysis by taking measurements, such as of the diameter of a blood spatter (drops), to figure out what happened. How do you think the diameter of spatter changes as liquid travels different distances? Find out by using some fake blood in this activity and trying your hand at collecting evidence!

MATERIALS

- Measuring spoons
- Cornstarch
- Corn syrup
- Red food coloring (or another color of your choice)
- Water
- Fork or spoon for mixing
- Plastic wrap (optional)
- Sheet of cardboard (You will want a total surface of at least 4 square feet [0.37 sq m]. You can use multiple smaller sheets of cardboard instead of one large one. The cardboard should be able to lay flat and not have many folds.)
- Pencil or pen
- Medicine dropper
- Measuring tape
- Ruler with millimeter and centimeter marks
- Butcher paper or newspaper (optional)
- A helper
- A location to do your activity (It should be where the ground can be easily cleaned in case of spilling the fake blood. For example, concrete or linoleum may work well.)

PREPARATION

- Prepare the fake blood. Start by measuring out 2 tablespoons of cornstarch and placing them into the bowl.
- Thoroughly mix 2 tablespoons (30 ml) of water into the cornstarch.
- Add 4 tablespoons (60 ml) of corn syrup to the bowl and mix thoroughly. The mixture should be smooth.
- Mix in 1 teaspoon (5 ml) of red (or other color) food coloring. Stir until the mixture is a steady color.
- You should now have a small bowl of fake blood (or other liquid, if you prefer less gore!). If you will not be using it right away, cover the bowl (such as with plastic wrap) and set it aside for now.
- Be careful not to spill the fake blood on furniture or carpeting—it can stain! If it does spill, be sure to clean up the liquid immediately. (Before you lay down the cardboard you might also want to cover the ground where you will be doing the activity with butcher paper or lots of newspaper to help prevent stains.)

PROCEDURE

- Lay the sheet(s) of cardboard flat on the ground where you will do your activity (placing the extra paper below and surrounding if desired).
- Fill the medicine dropper with some fake blood or liquid and hold the dropper vertically 1 foot (30 cm) above the cardboard sheet. Have a helper use the measuring tape to make sure the end of the dropper is 1 foot (30 cm) above the sheet.
- Drop a single drop of fake blood onto the cardboard.

- Repeat this process at least four more times while holding the dropper over slightly different areas so that you have dropped a total of at least five drops onto the cardboard. (If any of the drops land on another drop or in a crease or fold on the cardboard, do not count them in your total of five.) Use a pencil or pen to label the five successful drops "1 foot" (30 cm) next to each of them on the cardboard. *Do all of the drops look similar in size?*

- Now have the helper use the measuring tape to make sure the end of the dropper is 3 feet (0.9 m) above the cardboard sheet. Drop a total of at least five drops from this new height, 3 feet (0.9 m) above the sheet, in different spots, only counting drops that don't land on other drops or in folds. Label these drops "3 feet" (0.9 m) on the cardboard. *Do these drops look larger or smaller than the drops made from 1 foot (30 cm)?*

- Lastly, have the helper use the measuring tape to make sure the end of the dropper is 5 feet (1.5 m) above the cardboard. (Have a taller helper hold the dropper that high if you need more height—or use a sturdy stepladder with a spotter.) Drop a total of at least five drops from this height, only counting drops that don't land on other drops or in folds. Label these drops "5 feet" (1.5 m) on the cardboard. *Do these drops look larger or smaller than the drops made from lower heights?*

- Let all of the drops dry, being careful not to disturb them. Note that the drops may look glossy and wet even after they have dried. You might want to add an extra drop on the cardboard somewhere that you can test (by touching it) to see when the drops have completely dried.

- After all the drops have dried, measure the diameter of each one in centimeters or millimeters. Take your measurements very carefully, there may be only small, but measurable, differences between the drops. Write the diameters on the cardboard next to the drops.

- *How did the drops' diameters change as the fake blood (or liquid) was dropped from different heights? How do you think your results could help a forensic scientist figure out what happened at a crime scene?*

SCIENCE FAIR IDEA

Instead of dropping the fake blood straight down, try dropping it at angles to the ground or dropping it while moving the dropper in a certain direction. Be sure to do this in a location that can be accidentally stained with fake blood! *How does this change the size and shape of the drop's impact and where the spatter ends up?*

SCIENCE FAIR IDEA

Repeat this activity over other surfaces, such as newspaper, printer paper, parchment paper, paper towels, butcher paper, or wood, being careful to avoid surfaces that should not be stained. *How do your results change when using different surfaces?*

SCIENCE FAIR IDEA

In this activity you tried dropping fake blood from 1 foot (30 cm), 3 feet (0.9 m), and 5 feet (1.5 m). Try repeating the activity but use different heights and then graph your results. *What kind of graph does the data make? What kind of mathematical correlation is there between the height the drop is dropped from and its diameter on the surface it impacts?*

OBSERVATIONS AND RESULTS

Did the diameter of the fake blood drops increase as the dropping height increased?

You should have seen that the drops made from dropping the fake blood at 5 feet (1.5 m) were the largest in diameter whereas the drops made from dropping the fake blood at 1 foot (30 cm) had the smallest diameters. The differences in diameters, however, were likely small, with the 5-foot (1.5 m) drops possibly about 12 millimeters in diameter, the 1-foot (30 cm) drops around 10 mm in diameter and the 3-foot (0.9 m) drops in between—close to 11 mm. By understanding how blood spatter increases in diameter as the dropping height is increased, forensic scientists can better figure out what happened at some crime scenes. What other type of science could studying this sort of liquid behavior help with?

CLEANUP

When you are done with this activity, clean up any mess you may have made and dispose of your cardboard.

Saucy Science

Comparing Cranberry Condiments

BE THANKFUL FOR YOUR TASTE BUDS IN THIS THANKSGIVING TEST!

PROJECT TIME

30 minutes

KEY CONCEPTS

Cooking
Food
Heat
Polymer
Pectin

Does your family have jellied cranberry sauce with Thanksgiving dinner? Jellied cranberries are thick and retain the shape of the mold in which they are placed, which might mean a turkey-shaped mold or even the shape of the can if you use one of the popular canned kinds. Taking a bite of wiggly jellied cranberries can be a fun addition to a delicious meal, but cranberries can also be served as a liquid-like sauce. Both versions use the same ingredients, so what makes one turn into a gelatin whereas the other stays more fluid? To find out, try out this holiday-flavored science activity!

BACKGROUND

Cranberry sauce can be served either as a gooey liquid or as a solid jelly. The jellied version is solid enough to retain the shape of the container in which it's placed whereas the sauce version is much more fluid. The difference between the fluid sauce and the jelly versions comes down to pectin.

Pectin is a natural polymer—a series of molecules that attach to one another to form long chains. It is found between plant cells and within their cell walls. Pectin helps "glue" the plant cells together, keeping their tissues firm. And in cooked cranberries as well as in other fruit jams and jellies this pectin can help stick the cooked fruit together to form a solid jelly. When cranberries are cooked, their pectin polymers tangle and interact, forming a net that traps dissolved sugar molecules so they can't flow. This creates a firm shape. Cranberries naturally contain a lot of pectin, which helps keep the berries nice and firm. This extra pectin gets released when they are cooked. But what determines if the resulting cranberry sauce is liquid or jelly?

MATERIALS

- Two 12 ounce bags of fresh or frozen whole cranberries
- Colander
- 2 cups of granulated white sugar
- Water
- Measuring cup
- Pot, at least 4-quart (3.8 l) capacity
- Heat-resistant, long-handled spoon for mixing on the stove
- Stove
- Candy thermometer (It's highly recommended to use one that comes with a clip to attach it to the side of the pot.)
- Watch or timer
- Ladle
- Four ramekins or other small, heat-resistant containers, such as mugs or a muffin tin (They should each hold at least 3/4 cup, and be the same size and shape.)
- Butter knife and plates (optional)

PREPARATION

- If you are using frozen cranberries, thaw them beforehand.
- Pour two packages of cranberries into a colander. Rinse the cranberries; throw away any that are squishy rather than firm; drain thoroughly and set them aside.
- Make sure an adult helps with making the cranberry samples on the stove. When it is on the stove, the cranberry mixture will be very hot and prone to splattering. Be cautious when stirring—if the mixture gets on your skin, it could burn.

PROCEDURE

- Add 2 cups (0.5 l) of water and 2 cups of sugar to the pot. If you are using a candy thermometer with a clip, attach the thermometer to the side of the pot. Heat the pot on a stove-top burner, adjusting the burner to medium-high heat. Stir the water and sugar mixture until all the sugar is dissolved.
- Add the cranberries and stir occasionally. After a couple of minutes, the cranberries should start popping open. *What does this sound and look like?*
- Keep stirring until you can count slowly to five without hearing another cranberry pop open. What is the temperature of the mixture? If the temperature is below about 210°F (99°C), continue stirring and keeping an eye on the temperature. You'll need to keep stirring the mixture almost continuously, and you may need to turn the heat up to high to reach the 210°F (99°C) mark. (Note: Far above sea level, water boils at lower temperatures—about 203°F (95°C) at an elevation of 1 mile (1.6 km). As such, if you live at a high elevation, your mixture might not reach 210°F (99°C) and you should aim for a slightly lower temperature.)

- Once the temperature reaches about 210°F (99°C) (or the equivalent for your elevation), start timing. *How do the cranberries look after three minutes? Are they mostly whole, completely unrecognizable from the rest of the sauce, or somewhere in between?* At this point, scoop out one ladle full of cranberry mixture and carefully pour it in a ramekin (or other small, heat-resistant container). *What is the consistency of the mixture you scooped out?*

- Continue stirring, timing, and observing the cranberry mixture. Remove another full ladle of cranberry mixture after seven minutes since you started timing. Pour it into a separate ramekin. *How do the cranberries look now? What is the mixture's consistency like?*

- In this same way, remove a full ladle of cranberry mixture at 11 minutes and another at 15 minutes since you started timing, putting each scoop into their own ramekin.

- *How do the cranberries look after 15 minutes of cooking compared with three minutes? How did the consistency of the cranberry mixture change over time as it was cooked? How do the colors of the mixtures compare with one another? Do you see a relationship between these observations and how long the cranberries were cooked?*

EXTRA

If you have time, let the cranberry sauce samples cool at least two hours at room temperature. After they've cooled unmold each sample onto a fresh plate by running a butter knife along the inside edges of the ramekin or container to gently loosen the cranberry mixture, placing a plate facedown on top of the ramekin and then flipping over the ramekin and plate together. *What is the color and consistency of the different samples once they've cooled? How do they compare with one another? Do any of them retain the molded shape of the ramekin, which means they're considered to be jellied cranberry sauce?*

EXTRA

Sugar plays an important part in allowing pectin molecules to find one another when cooking cranberries. To investigate this, try this activity again but this time try increasing and/or decreasing the amount of sugar you use. *What happens to the cranberry sauce's ability to solidify as you change the amount of sugar in the recipe?* Hint: If you're having trouble interpreting your results, you might also want to think about (or try discovering) what sugar does to the boiling point of water.

EXTRA

Try this activity with other fruits. *What other fruits have enough natural pectin to create solid gels?*

OBSERVATIONS AND RESULTS

Did the cranberry mixture that cooked the longest make the thickest and firmest jellied cranberry sauce? Did the one that was cooked for the shortest amount of time make a relatively runny, liquidlike cranberry sauce with whole cranberries still visible?

The longer the cranberries were heated in the hot liquid, the more they should have broken apart, which releases more and more pectin polymers into the water. The more the pectin polymers bind to one another, the greater the mixture's structure and firmness. (Also, water is released as steam while you cook the cranberries, which means that the longer they cook, the less water they hold.) Taken together, this is why the cranberry sauce that was cooked the longest should have been the thickest and had the fewest whole cranberries visible when it was hot and being stirred. It should also have been the firmest, thereby retaining its shape the best once cooled. On the other hand, the cranberry sauce that was cooked for just three minutes should have been the most liquidlike, with whole cranberries visible, when it was being prepared, and it should have been the thinnest sample once cooled. As you should have seen in this activity, jellied cranberry sauce (which retains its shape) can be made by cooking fluid cranberry sauce for a longer amount of time.

CLEANUP

You may enjoy a tasty snack of cranberry sauce!

THE SCIENTIFIC METHOD

The scientific method helps scientists—and students—gather facts to prove whether an idea is true. Using this method, scientists come up with ideas and then test those ideas by observing facts and drawing conclusions. You can use the scientific method to develop and test your own ideas!

Question: What do you want to learn? What problem needs to be solved? Be as specific as possible.
Research: Learn more about your topic and refine your question.
Hypothesis: Form an educated guess about what you think will answer your question. This allows you to make a prediction you can test.
Experiment: Create a test to learn if your hypothesis is correct. Limit the number of variables, or elements of the experiment that could change.
Analysis: Record your observations about the progress and results of your experiment. Then analyze your data to understand what it means.
Conclusion: Review all your data. Did the results of the experiment match the prediction? If so, your hypothesis was correct. If not, your hypothesis may need to be changed.

GLOSSARY

astronomer: A person who studies stars, planets, and other heavenly bodies.

carbohydrate: A nutrient in many types of food that the body uses as a source of energy.

correlating: Understanding how things relate to one another.

dense: Packed very closely together.

diameter: The distance from one side of a round object to another through its center.

dilute: To make thinner or less powerful by adding liquid.

dissolved: Mixed completely into a liquid.

fetus: A developing human from usually two months after conception to birth.

genetic: Relating to genes.

gore: Bloodiness or gruesomeness.

humid: Containing moisture.

malaria: A disease, or illness, usually spread by mosquito bites.

nuclear family: A family group that's made up of only parents and children.

nutritious: Containing things needed to grow and stay alive.

optional: Not required.

pathology: The study of the nature of diseases.

supervision: The act of watching and directing an activity.

well-ventilated: Airy or allowing good air flow.

ADDITIONAL RESOURCES

Books

Andrus, Abre. *Good Housekeeping Amazing Science: 83 Hands-on S.T.E.A.M Experiments for Curious Kids!* New York, NY: Hearst Home Kids, 2021.

Dingle, Adrian. *Awesome Chemistry Experiments for Kids: 40 STEAM Science Projects and Why They Work.* Emeryville, CA: Rockridge Press, 2021.

Morlock, Rachael. *Makerspace Projects for Understanding Plant Science.* New York, NY: Rosen Publishing Group, 2021.

Websites

Discovery Education
sciencefaircentral.com

Exploratorium
https://www.exploratorium.edu/search/science%20fair%20projects

Science Buddies
https://www.sciencebuddies.org/science-fair-projects/project-ideas/list

Science Fun

https://www.sciencefun.org/?s=science+fair

Videos

How to Cookie with Science
https://ny.pbslearningmedia.org/resource/cookie-with-science-reactions/cookie-with-science-reactions/

How to Grow Fluorescent Flowers
https://ny.pbslearningmedia.org/resource/fluorescent-flowers-reactions/fluorescent-flowers-reactions/

Publisher's note to educators and parents: Our editors have carefully reviewed these websites to ensure that they are suitable for students. Many websites change frequently, however, and we cannot guarantee that a site's future contents will continue to meet our high standards of quality and educational value. Be advised that students should be closely supervised whenever they access the internet.

INDEX